GW00418530

Other Exley Giftbooks:

The Fanatic's Guide to Love
Thinking of You
Love Quotations
Passion
True Love...
A Token of Love

Published simultaneously in 1997 by Exley Publications in Great Britain, and Exley Giftbooks in the USA.

12 11 10 9 8 7 6 5 4 3 2

ISBN 1-85015-803-7

A copy of the CIP data is available from the British Library on request.

Edited by Helen Exley.
Cartoons and text by Roland Fiddy.
Printed and bound in China.

Exley Publications Ltd., 16 Chalk Hill, Watford, Herts. WD1 4BN UK.
Exley Publications LLC, 232 Madison Avenue, Suite 1206,
NY 10016, USA.

I'm Missing You

CARTOONS BY Fudge

EXLEY
NEW YORK • WATFORD, UK

I miss you when
I think of the
distance between
us.

MISSING
YOU

I miss you when
I look out to sea

Missing
You

I miss you when I walk in the country

I miss you when
I am alone.

MISSING YOU

I miss you
at nights

M I S S I N G Y O U

I miss you when
I hear our music

MISSING YOU:

I miss you when
I'm working....

MISSING YOU
MISSING YOU
MISSING YOU
MISSING YOU
MISSING YOU
MISSING YOU
MISSING YOU

...I miss you
when I'm not

Missing you

I miss you when
a plane flies by

Missing you

I miss you when
the sun is shining

MISSING YOU

I miss you when I
gaze at the stars..

MISSING YOU

I miss you on
our special days

Missing you

Until we
meet again...